Birthmark

Poetry chapbooks by Christina Hennemann

Leafing (Cerasus Poetry, 2024)
Witch/Womb (BookHub Publishing, 2024)
Illuminations at Nightfall (Sunday Mornings at the River, 2022)

Birthmark

Christina Hennemann

Shearsman Books

First published in the United Kingdom in 2025 by
Shearsman Books Ltd
PO Box 4239
Swindon
SN3 9FN

Shearsman Books Ltd Registered Office
30–31 St. James Place, Mangotsfield, Bristol BS16 9JB
(this address not for correspondence)

EU AUTHORISED REPRESENTATIVE:
Lightning Source France
1 Av. Johannes Gutenberg, 78310 Maurepas, France
Email: compliance@lightningsource.fr

www.shearsman.com

ISBN 978-1-84861-985-2

CONTENTS

Maybe I am a maned wolf
lanky, tremulous legs
as if I stepped in something
knee deep and dark it makes me
look as though I can dance or
keep it all close to my torso
this is why I skitter when alarmed

— Nidhi Zak/Aria Eipe,
'Self-portrait, with shyness',
Auguries of a Minor God

Auguries of Migration

It was summer, before the scent of rain.
And the swallows fled the farmhouse
quicker than you, spoon-feeding milk.
You sang, bent over my crib, that lies live
shorter in the small mouth of a girl,
while the toads outside kept croaking,
prophesying the fatal snow of night
until dawn rose over the rippled pond.

*

The day after you were gone.
I couldn't find you, would have gone
insane behind the curtains, had you not left
your fingerprint on the smudged window,
pointing at our sighing plum tree, bee-stung
and purple with July's kiss. No trace
of Hungarian Yews moaning under snow,
cones heavy with sleet and ache—

only a garden, & bathing in light.

Lunchbox

You sliced the mealy apples from Aldi
into eight pieces, five days a week.
I didn't like the taste, but I loved

their half-moon shape. You braided
my hair, tugged on my thick strands
so they'd stay in place, my scalp burning

with your worries. The girls in school
had sesame toasties, cookies, pitted
cherries fitting the tips of their tongues,

their hair shiny like a golden coin. I wanted
toasties, too, but you bought rye bread, ten
cents per sole, you put your foot down.

Please buy Nutella instead of Nussetti, just one time.
You wouldn't believe I'd taste the difference,
your hazel eyes a shade lighter

when I passed the blind test at my aunt's.
One more time, you laughed, incredulous.
But still, you'd spread Nussetti on those soles,

counting your copper coins on the kitchen table
as my tongue grew sour to you, only my strict
plait dragging me down from my high horse.

Prozaic Skies

Pink hearts in a window sparkling frantically; rain cold in February's
riptide. I will look every day for dog poo waiting on the sidewalk
and its cunning ploy to stain my steps: sharp yells and your pushing
will follow me as I grow up, afraid to put my foot in it, no longer seeing
the sky above. Your sky is grey, weighted with acid rain, and worms
lurking to creep up from the earth. Stray cats pacing behind bins.
You don't believe in Valentine's, but love is all around you, just stop
forcing it into a heart. At home, my mother knows. She knows I'm here.
She knows I'm eight years old and picking out a gift for her. For you.
With clean soles and unspeckled legs despite the poo and the puddles.
You request red wrapping paper with white hearts and your fingers
around my wrist are cold and damp. Just like the weather, the clouds
pushing further and blocking the sun, streets covered in muck and then
snow, falling softly as tiny crystals, latching on to our coats, glistening
for a moment before they melt.

Toy for a Rebel Girl

He was not my favourite toy.
Ugly, wrapped in his grey fur coat,
glass eyes mirroring my sulks.
Two teeth waved like white flags,
hiding lips: if he spoke he'd surely lisp.
His body was stiff, tough muscles
ready to beat and punch and run,
a bow drawn to the maximum point
of tension before the arrow shoots out.
His leather-snout crumpled and faded
in the salty drops from my nose.
He didn't have a name as he had no
parents, so I christened him with the power
of my flesh and skin and sour fervour:
Stone-Grater, that should be his name,
strong enough to bite through rock,
until he found a way to the sun-bound
meadow where even antiheroes play.

Lilith

versus the Code of Hammurabi (written ca. 1750 BC)

I left Eden when the grass turned envy-yellow and snakes
crawled on open wounds around the apple tree, flesh dripping red

like forbidden fruit. On leaving, I was thrust into space.
Now I'm the lunar apogee farthest from Earth, a void space

you named Black Moon. I'm the death of space and stars, darkness
in the pit of your stomach and hole in your heart. I'm not

a planet, not even a place, I'm merely the idea of a God too weak to love.
From eons away, I'm hovering over Adam's throne like a ghost,

and I'm telling you this: no demon has ever drowned. Because I dry
their rivers by drinking. I can hold more water than God's flooded earth.

In the book, ink on paper, I shall own Adam and call his walls my home.

Weeding

My father was obsessed with weeding:
patio weeder in hand, no morsel of moss
        in the cracks between paving stones
        escaped his picking and plucking.
And the lawn, *oh!* What uproar at the sight
of a dandelion leaf, budding, screaming
        the arrival of a sunny blot on the green—
        Ha! Fierce cut with the trowel, uprooted soil,
his hands could rest then for a while,
steadied when all was in order: *pure*,
        overlooking the blood-brown wounds, until
        he spotted the blooming red between my lips,
          growing louder and wild, stubborn roots

hiding cunningly in cerebral crevices.
        He cut, pulled, dug deep unremittingly to contain

        the plague, but the weeds always won the fight.

I never asked him why he did it, his answer
          was planted within me

      from the beginning:
        Life is chaos, and the tormented exorcism

of fear.

Self-Portrait of a Mother, 1863

after Frederick Walker, 'The Lost Path' (1863) & Annemarie Ní Churreáin

God, I rise from my sickbed.
I rise from my seat by the fire
and shuffle through snow.
I rise from the icy path, from pride.
I rise from the winter-hard day
to lift my child up to the stars.
I rise from hunger and thirst,
from blisters and bleeding mouths,
no longer fearing canines, skeletal eyes.
I rise from the darkest woods
to raise my child as one of the moon.
I rise from my feet to fly with the winged wolf
through unbending crowns of trees,
and carry my baby to the light-adorned gate.
I rise from sin and mend my wounds
with leather and fur, let the wolf
lick my baby's bones
free from skin, wrap them in wings.
I rise to the laws of the sky, where angels
sing rain clouds into cirrus,
and eye to eye with my child,
my frostbitten hands clasp.

Map, in Parts

after Olga Tokarczuk

In a workshop I draft my poetic
map of home & find Agatha of Sicily: virgin,

whore, captive, saint. The Etna's lava fell
asleep in the girl's veil. Her breasts

sit in a bakery for sale. She would not
love a man for the price of a lie. Rebel-

girl admonished saint. I was christened
in St. Agatha Church & grew up

on Agatha Street, loop of tar, plunged
between fields. Red-brick bourgeoisie. Suburban

cul-de-sac. Centre of my 90s girl universe—

↑
Oak woods for treasure-hunting
bird feathers. Beyond, the fields

where I pluck strawberries
in summer. Year after year

the fields shrink as a new estate
shoots from the ground. From the seesaws

in Kindergarten I watch concrete
conquer pastures and grow

into the sky. This part is threatened
by greed, and Agatha blesses it with an elm leaf.

←

Playground, soccer pitches, riding
school, lined by the river Werse

flowing along mazes of fields. Under roofs
of leaves, my best friend and I steal corn, stuffing

our pants, fleeing from the farmer's blood-
hound. Smoke the cobs on father's barbecue.

This is the part endangered by losing
oneself in summer, and Agatha blesses it with an acorn.

→

After school I spend my pocket money
in the copy shop on sour

gums & Diddl stationery to deal
for rarer prints. Sometimes I cross

the big bridges over canal & Autobahn
into the city centre, to crush

my piggy bank for Westlife CDs. Later
I learn on a school trip

about the anabaptists who rotted
in St. Lambert's cages & the peace

of Westphalia in our town hall. Beyond
the Western walls: gallow's heath.

This part is threatened by gluttony
and Agatha blesses it with snakeskin.

↓

Gate to fear: the streets of Osttor
a concrete riddle to be walked

only in the company of father. Men
in tracksuit pants smoke,

leaning against their barracks. Once I find
a syringe stuck in the cracks

of the pavement. A gravelly path
opens into lush fields, leads to my mother's

favourite flower shop. This part is tempted
by pride, and Agatha blesses it with a dandelion.

*

Centre of my 90s girl universe: street
blessed with Agatha's name, where girls

play like boys: I kick
the ball on the street, graze

my knees on the hot tar
named after her. Blood as mark

of pride: wild witchling
climbing trees & cars. Tie

the swing's metal strings
around the beam, watch

the street from higher up, peeling
plasters off my skin: let the blood

crust like cooling lava.

Party Politics

I don't mind being stirred, but I refuse to be shaken
Herr Habeck has significantly reduced his shower time
since the outbreak of the war my legs are stems
and my toes roots drilling into the small patch of earth
I'm squatting on, my German potatoes, my Irish potatoes,
and I don't give a damn about the political porridge,
Mister Martin says all sectors will have to stretch themselves
to meet emission targets we pay the price when we want to stay
warm, and my thoughts race to the little girl
red-cheeked in sandals and swinging dress
that licked thick ice cream at the sizzling funfair,
or red-cheeked in her penguin pyjamas, sleepyhead
under blazing hot heaters after a snowball fight.
My brows furrow thinking of the serious affairs that followed
and shaded her cherry blossoms, her soil, her infectious laugh,
lungs filling with acid and dooming dis-ease.
Herr Habeck is sour
Mister Martin is worried
I'm balancing on a leaf of grass with my left big toe—
potatoes cold and dark in the ground,
casting the spell: *We are of the trees, and our shadows*
reach beyond party politics.

Solitary/Riverbed

On the day you were born
the morning haze came down
and veiled the pier like a bride,
innocent kiss on sea-worn bricks.
Your mother bled a river, eskering
over gravel and sand; muddy birth.
The Little Egret sat on tortoise rock,
her white plumage a diamond on grey.
Egrets hunt alone, unless starving,
the dark beak ready to lunge and wound.
She chased the twinning thief away,
took the whole seabed in her reign.
And in a capsule of nine months gone,
your mother held a freckled hand,
belly-inhaled the misty morning for you,
as the Egret's wings pierced the fog,
sharp with her oath to catch a fish.

The Garden That Never Belonged to Us

The peacock strutted along the fence, his blue
shimmer menacing in the summer sun,
and screeched at the polished

windows; fix his eyes on my gate
of hands clutching my pulse, stare
as if trying to give me a message. But I did not

understand. In a quick flutter
of courage I banged my fist against the window
to chase him away. He retreated, hurt

gleaming in his dark eye as he stalked
to the pansies, rubbed his cheek
against their blossoms. I let my hands sink

and he shrieked at my act
of small relief; spread his feather
dress, all his green-blue eyes on me,

accusing. My mother came, secateurs
trembling in her hands. Side by side
we sat on the couch, watching the peacock

until we fell asleep. When we woke up, he was
gone. For months we were certain
he'd died, until he strode through the garden

again like it belonged to him, perplexed
by our presence in the house. His dress
of a thousand eyes, warning us

that we could not
stay. That we still had enough
eyes to see the path ahead of us.

At the Dinner Table, Across from Depression

Your eyes pricked me until my skin
leathered, like a cow's. I learned

to focus on the wall above your head, on the tiny
scar in the red paint, blank white space,

as your moustache wrapped around your fork, no
teeth showing but I knew they were there, hiding

like a cat's claws. I would've laughed if I didn't feel
so heavy in my cow's body, chewing with plate-eyes

to pretend I wasn't thinking. Just ruminating. The scar
danced on your head the longer I stared. With closed

eyes I saw a sun in a puddle of mud. Some days
you knifed me with questions and the answers

had to be precise. So precise that they cut
in my gum and my food burned in the wound. Other days

you fixed your eyes on the window, scanning
the hedges and planning perhaps where to cut

fresh shoots, or maybe it was something else.
I could eat then, my head bent

over the plate. Fork for fork I shovelled
as if I wasn't a cow, but a snake, swallowing

whole — as long as you didn't look.

Stoner, or: My Father's Shrinking

after John Williams & Bruno Schulz

Once upon a time, my father was a giant.
Bear paws holding my head, rocking my cradle.
I nestled into his palm like a chestnut after the feeding,
later he put a mahogany desk in his study
from where I'd look up at him.

He first shrank to half his size when my mother came in.
Her laugh was a battering ram, and my desk turned
pink, wrapped in ribbons he barely recognised
my smile. He let mother love me
the way she knew — stuck in my throat.

When body grew tall and branched, he almost disappeared.
His flesh dried, the bones cracked, and one day
I found him folded in the pages of his book. There was no
poetry on his skin, merely scattered words like love
and regret. I tore him out and dunked him in wine.

Cherry and soaked he tasted sweet against my tongue.
He wilted like a leaf pressed between anthologies, saw me
blossom in that light of the desk lamp; the raw and red
in our eyes locked one last time. He crumpled to dust.
The bottle ripped my lips open, leaked into paper towels.

"He was always busy with work," my mother sighed,
"All I'll have left are his blank pages."

Sankt Bernhard

for Opa

Rugged skin strapped over ploughs: earth-stained
your hands cave my face like the eyrie its egg.

On this field you're the German shepherd
counting sheep. In Oma's bed you're the lamb

with blue eyes, no longer growing
gnarls, erratic branches. *Why are gooseberries*

called thornberries in German? I ask, nesting my hand
in yours. *We put food on the table,* you say, *ora et labora.*

Gretel Without Hänsel

I trace each step with sugar canes,
bind my breasts with cloth: the wolves
and woods won't see me then.

Mother says *steal pearls and meat.*
Father twirls my plaits around his fingers.
My hair grows long and brittle, back
bends like old gingerbread.

I leave Hänsel with the witch. Her eyes
fatten his finger. They dance around
the bun in the oven as I stuff

my pockets without being caught—
but wolves smell fear
through sugarcoats.

Parent-Hood

after Dorothy Cross, 'Shark Lady in a Balldress' (1988)

You have always been dangerous, femme fatale
and Captain Mammarica melted as one and all.
My eyelids lift under the touch of your hands,
I poke your paper bag breasts with my nose.
They crumble and tumble and belly-down,
my lips find a nipple & suckle the milk-
like liquid, harden my bones as sun
streams in through the gap between
the blinds, swinging curtains part
ways and reveal the leak of light.
Vigour, life, a rush of blood
& bile in my limbs: I kick
your cushions and rustle
the bags, hide my head
inside and tear them
open like gifts.
You chuckle
and nudge
my nose
with
your
sausage-
finger,
dent
my
cheeks
until I
gurgle
with
joy.

Mutter/Kuchen

"Mutterkuchen" is German for placenta, and the word's individual parts translate as mother (Mutter), and cake (Kuchen).

You gained five stones with me, I thickened
your bones, you told me with leaden brows.

Nougat and cake bewitched your hazel eye
and full lip with me starving your placenta.

Then I burst out of you, fat and greedy, you fed me
the sweet tooth, too: each year you made that choc-dripping

gateau for my birthday, seven dwarfs of sugar dough
cheering me on— I was only Snow White until I dug in.

You never lost the croissants you puffed up for me, and then
my sister came: buttered by two sweet daughters you gave in,

tossed out the scales and spreadsheets, carefree and almost joy
in the art of baking cakes, lifting yourself up to new tiers,

while I measured the width of my waist and thighs,
weighed your creations in my belly after each celebration.

Today, no longer cursing my cravings, I'd get on a plane
to sit with you and feast on your birthday gateau. I can swallow

the love you fed me from the very first day, and every soft pouch
of yours is warmer than all the candles on the cake.

*

Diary Notes from a Young Self

after Edna St. Vincent Millay

What: sealskin, oil poured over lamp, branch bursting with olives, fingers circling buttons & bellies, feral eyes between thighs

lips: arrow piercing philtrum under perfect Cupid's bow, breath over feathery down, clicking of tongue against water, melting glacier racing breast-wards, & always Hara Hachi Bu

my: warmth left on bedsheets, pillow dented from weight of thoughts, coat left hanging over chair, clothes strewn across tile, coals cackling

lips: melted, moist, & strings weaving into knots, dew drops hanging from rose blossom, dripping

have: ice bucket to sit in overwhelmed, whips lashing across back for every thought of sex, axe splitting strawberry & blood sprinkled over thighs, honey coating throat, can't swallow

kissed: finger stuck in a vacuum, bitten by incisors, bombing the cream cake with cotton ball, picking up pieces on all fours, knees bent & bruised

and: rubbing gum against sandpaper, quest for father, plum crushed to juice, then liquored & burned, smoke wafting in air, up towards a red sky

where: back to back & eye to eye, head in sand & sole to sky, torn up, face the clearing: feeling sonder, sonderbar, besonders absonderlich

and: peeling skin from bone, quest for girl, rattling skeleton in closet, open the door & shut the mouth, claw toes into rug, throw an eye in every direction, seeing it all go

why: I am—

Affirmations for a Social Climber

Forget winter moths, dead and alive:
clothes munched into rags, warmth
fleeing through holes

and seams. Forget the axe in the bird
house: tits don't need mouldy seeds
scattered in a pigeon's

shithole. Forget dripping summer
sweat: sausages must be smoked, skin
thickens when barbecued

on coughing coals. Forget greasy fingers:
fed with Aldi's fries and ham, oil stains
on glasses train a tight grip

on water. Forget yellow stains
in underpants: beer urges
urination, laundry liquid is cheaper

than toilet paper. Forget him peeing
in the dark at night: money's an ocean
receding to flush ashore another place.

I wait in that other place.

Sadhbh,

the doe herd gathered for the last jump
across the freezing stream. Bare shrubs
glistened with frost and on the ground
lay smashed pearls of deadly nightshade.
The deer tripped on mud, their wet noses

sniffing poison, or tossed wrapping paper
and plastic bottles. Why didn't you come?
Last summer I walked around the lake
with you. Unflinching. The batteries
in your torch died when the stars came out.

You pointed at the matriarch, she watched us
from behind a tree. A pine. Who was
pining? You hated the cold. Winter's
stiff silence. Sadhbh, when the first doe
turned back, from the other side, I swear

her eyes met mine. My ice-blue ones.
The stream was still. Frozen over. One
by one they disappeared into the woods
with smudged hooves, soft and fading
kissing sounds. I've never seen the mud so sad.

Britney's Bargain

Put on your red hold-ups, he said.

He thrust me into his vastest sky:
I was a supernova,
and sinking without gravity.
I wish I'd had a lifebelt at least, like Saturn.

I don't want you to keep it, he said.

My guts were a spiral, narrowing,
twisted in his fouling promises.
He held many strings around his thumb,
none tied to his sinewy calves.

I would end up resenting you, he said.

My cheeks were glowing scarlet,
shiny apple of love and lust.
He was not the first man to hate me,
who dug his pinky in my aorta.

My freedom supersedes everything, he said.

I slipped out of my hold-ups,
knotted them into a string,
hung them around my larynx
so I wouldn't burden him.

I said nothing.

Bonding

I woke and found the space beside me empty, pillow hollowed
in the shape of your head, blanket draped over waning body

warmth. Oxytocin rushed through my veins, my heart swelling
and aching. I told myself then that the longing will pass—

Biochemical chaos caused by the brain, a primal tool
of attachment, luring you to procreate, you animal.

I dressed and left in a hurry, to the beach to find myself
again, between grains of sand that rub my calloused heels.

I will be here when the wave breaks, you said, *I'm not afraid*
of things that come crashing. I saw you duck, dive, splutter,

until you mastered the art of being carried. You didn't lose
yourself in the sea. I stood still until my eyes dried. My feet

carried me back to bed, hormones levelled in a low tide & you
knitted into sheets, your eyes un-braiding the knot in my throat.

Lying beside you, I imagine I quoted Vuong: *Eviscerate me,*
and I'll tell you the truth— to master the art of being an ocean.

Self-Portrait of a Daughter, 1963

after Gloria Steinem & Annemarie Ní Churreáin

Mother, I've fallen from your chest.
I've fallen into cushion-clouds
plump with crystal water.
I've fallen in my whitest dress.
I've fallen on my back
like a beetle with a breast-shaped weight.
I've fallen into freedom and light,
to spread my legs wide open and breathe.
I've fallen to smoke and tar my voice.
I've fallen for pearls and plums
to rid me of my womb's fetters
and lose my heart in bedsheets of skin.
I've fallen to smirk at those who pray
in the palace where blood-gold and stones
build themselves up for herniation.
I've fallen for bunny tails on tree trunks,
fur felted with mud and moss
without questioning the holiness of grass.
I've fallen to dig my heels into the earth,
from the hull of spoon-deep black liquor,
and I look for you here, in my bell-like laugh,
asking you to chime.

Hades Gothic

after Sarah Ellen Lundy, 'Palmate v Point' & 'Every Woman Is An Eyeland' (2023)

Eye hear you, every woman is an eyeland, my I's
fixed on upturned earth, palms open for soil & antlers
point at the skull soaring above my grave. Frost is my blood
& fire my bones, starlights for petalled antlers, I'm flowerful, skeletal
skullflower stung with sun, casting her shadows on me,
periosteum. Moonshine combs violet veins, branching into leafless
trees. Eye feel you, she went cold as eyes when he spat
his gaze under her skin, runny rivers & blue-blooded seas. This summer
is skating on frozen rain, last winter was corpses roasting on coals—
they howled at Mars for snow, at Venus for flames, danced
in a circle, clattering cartilage, I-balls rolling around in cleavages
like lost marbles, empty sockets, staring sockets, seeking
sockets, touching teeth: my sundial stops on spleen.

Seductive Blonde Gone Savage

MTV screams from the screen, sugar pop and strings
strewn across the floor, knotted knickers. You stumble
to the cellar to steal a bottle of red and I shut the door,
turn the key. Trap— a coal-black bunker
is a cramping muscle. I toss my hair into snakes
& Britney twirls her locks around her finger.

Knock knock, bang bang, you seek my salvation,
my soiled laugh summons shock waves through the slit
under the door. I see you're still naked down there.
Thinking of sipping the wine I'm lured in,
fork my tongue and hiss into the keyhole
& Britney licks her lips, shakes her hips.

I snake the door open and you burst out, sore
like a bitten fox but not broken, not you, you hero.
Souris, mon amour, it was only a silly joke, the fear
on your face fading, you're getting the hang of me.
I circle you and rip the bottle from your hands
& Britney blinks with her bedroom eyes.

Rebel bi Orgasm

Run: swirl up sand until your feet soak,
weed pools between your legs, see—
a goat swimming to your rescue.

Grab it by the horns and pull
yourself into the sea, you don't need
a lifeboat, plunged between animal fur.

Feel how hot you can quiver in cool splash,
and you had told yourself you couldn't
love, swallow salty gulps and giggle.

The goat drags you on its back and there,
you're floating far away from land,
frantic fingers tickling a golden horizon.

You hear yourself sing pebbles
from the hollows of your lungs, see—
you're free, falling for the hymn in waves.

This two-headed creation wasn't made
by God, it was you all along, splitting
triangle, esker running between your thighs.

You are the bones and the goat is
blood, rushing towards an opening,
I've just died, I've just been born.

Tale of Love Spells and Other Monsters

after the Chinese tale "Li Ji Slays the Giant Serpent"

Once upon a time, he devoured
young maidens. He tells me the tale,
yet I throw myself at him, fire-cheeked.

Eight maidens fell into his hands,
wrapped in hexes sung as lullabies, until
he swallowed them whole with starving eyes.

I am the ninth maiden, pond of a mouth,
staring at blinding-sharp fate: quicksilver
love running in my veins, but I grab hold

of his sword in my heart and tear it out,
bury it deep in his ribcage, blood filling
the blade's finely engraved *forever yours*.

Nesting Doll: Venus von Willendorf

Formed from limestone in lustful hands,
lips creased in a smile, be still
Goddess of Sex, arch your back.

Where is your home? Lost
wanderer, like Sarah Baartman
ogled in glossy skin, then bare bones.

Men crawl at your feet and moan
in slavish awe, you throw eyes of mud
against their throbbing loose end.

Women cry out: *melon belly!*
Obscene behind! But your beauty's
a peony, fragile in their dirty hands.

Your thighs are stems, uprooted
from your land; eyes roll
on your petals like lost marbles.

You ache to go home, to rest
in a hill's dark bosom, unseen—
Goddess of Sex, watch your back.

Canine

The male gorilla has much larger canines
than the female. Not merely functional teeth
for tearing, but a threatening gesture. *Cuspids,*
eye teeth, vampire fangs— names for a blood-
thirsty animal. That's how I caught you,
roaming the beach, canine teeth glimmering
under the silver sky. I recognised myself
in your grin. Remember how we both bared
our fangs, prowled on quiet paws, ready
to lunge at any moment? What you gave me
wasn't mash and butter, its substance sinews
and meat and salt. It hit me right to the bone
and marrow, sharp & leaving a bite on my neck—
a birthmark.

Tidal

I moulded myself
into a vacuum, a sucking space. I gave
the void legs to carry itself to your doorstep,
and dug my anchor into your heart: a cave
of gravel, and unravelled by the tides.

I moulded myself
into a curve at night, wide and bending
at the flailing of your limbs. I folded
back into dark matter as to not disturb your sleep.
My anchor came loose and dangled in a shallow tide.

I mould myself
into an ocean-moon: I wax and wane and die. I give
the void a face to look at you from a sharper angle,
and plant my anchor inside myself: an urchin
fort with thorns, and carried by the tides.

I remember you now as a wave-whisperer.
You smoothed a whole ocean, then buried
the glass beneath the foam you gathered inside your lungs.
From this standpoint your feet blur against the sea—
up above, a heron glides through the sun-split air.

The Pole Dancer Sees Cupid in the Mirror

for Kira

[Note: Cupid No Hands is a pole dance move]

Girl with dream of wings: limbs   take flight
& don't   be bitten.   You once read in a book
that women lie   in the eye of the beholder.
So you started to dance   in front of a mirror
smeared with sweat   and fingerprints.

Girl with dream of sky: a pole rose   from cracks
in dusty laminate   asking you to climb. You read
your Modern Witch Tarot & pulled   the Hanged
Woman— you saw yourself then   upside down
in a bind   battling gravity   with your dancer smile.

Girl with dream of sun: morning-soaked   skirt
trailed behind you like wings. You read in a book
that the devil's snake   eats women who dance
on a pole.   So you wound yourself around
in the shape of a star   blinding the snake.

Girl with dream of sleep: inner   thighs
pink like a tongue   screeching from heights
before you landed   soft   like the green
feather you hid in a book   you read
as a child— *Li Ji Slays the Giant Serpent.*

Girl with dream of earth: with blistered   hands
you wrapped your guts   in a bundle & dropped
them on stage   for your wounds   to breathe.
The books by women   told you nothing
about falling on your knees   until they bleed.

Girl waking from dream: fingers   run
over spine— the books you read about love
promised you wings   but the snake came
& clipped them   before   you'd fly.
You climb the pole: hold on with your legs

& spread   your arms   look
in the mirror: no wings   no hands
to hold you   just you   rooted
around the pole   & isn't that love
isn't that all   the love —

Cleopatra's Flashlight

As if foreshadowed, it then happened some nights
after your boyfriend said I had that Slavic poise,

and mine discovered your Vampire teeth. Girls' night
in: we stripped naked on your bed and you covered

your breasts, laughing away at those tiny
tents that I saw as pyramids. My udders

were wobbling across the bedsheet.
Our lips brushed against each other

as though hollow eggshells wanting a yolk.
You wound your legs around mine to hide

what they wanted to see most, we assumed,
and I held my breath, for that was all I had.

The overexposed photograph showed four legs
and milk-breasts trining pharaohs. It was just a game

to turn them on, we said, we know what boys want,
and I almost forgot my shame, my swelling. Maybe

our tongues were actually touching then. I can't
remember at all that time we drank Palma Nights

and made out in the fields. You ripped off my lips,
I tasted blood. Pooled between my thighs you forgot

to take a pic. It didn't matter much, I said,
it was just another hot story for the boys.

November Bed

All the way through the bleeding
he held my pain: sucking & swallowing
like the Daylily that dries up floods.

He held my hand and felt my forehead,
locked his glassy gaze on mine for signs of fever.

Later, crouched on the toilet alone, I could still
hear his footsteps on the stairs,

fetching water and pills, opening windows.
The wallowing strings inside my body loosened then,

and an orange seed (so the doctor said)
squeezed its way out to sip soiled waters.

After, I drank from the glass he held against my lips,
my head toppled into the valley of his shoulder.
In there, his heart drummed louder than ultrasound,

and I wanted to remember that the most.

Sunrise Over Mussenden Temple

i.m. Frideswide Mussenden

Take my boots, grass-wet and sunken.
Take the dust from my pebble-sealed hands.

Every fog-winged story *muss enden*.

Whisper my name at the sea falling from the window.
Whisper my red husks in your wife's hair.

Every love too far from shore

Rip my dresses and sew them into quilts.
Rip its seams when The Tempest is soaked in moonlight.

Every diamond-troubled life

Forget the colour of my hair, remember my ashes on the beach.
Forget my temple, leave it to the wind to drag it downhill.

Your sun-eclipsing search for heaven

Watch stones topple down and crash into waves.
Watch them know better than us holding on to water.

Me braiding strands of wind into my plait *muss enden*.

Let the books go. Let me go.
Open the curtains, let sunlight in—

Orion the Hunter

He poured me a red river, gushed
all over my sore synapses,
and chained me up with a golden
necklace, glowing with shiny blood
diamonds.

I tripped over his rocks and slipped
on rotten cherries,
but he glistened in the moonlight.

When the river dried up, I fell
asleep, feverish and foul.
He picked me up and decorated
my burning neck with pearls,
placed a shell on my bellybutton.

His kiss smelled of cosmic dust.
I withered in the black hole
in the corner of his smile,
but his stars sparkled and glittered.

(I bathe my lips in a blue river; I am—
sober.)

Poetry Submission

Dear poetry editor,
when you read my submission of three poems
think of me dumping a heavy metal box labelled
– *TRAUMA* –
in front of your crammed desk with a bang,
and when you suspiciously open the box,
think of unpacking the dusty creepy skeleton model
your science teacher used to explain human bone structure
and skeletal abnormalities while nobody listened,
as paper planes soared in the air high on suppressed laughter.
Think of pulling out the creased letter enclosed in the rib cage,
unfolding the sheet and discovering a clumsy blob of ink—
that was me pouring my pain on the page,
for you to consider if it's legible enough,
if I've crawled deep enough into the darkness,
and dragged out just enough dirt to intrigue you,
but not quite as much as to put you off in disgust,
as I need you to take part of my ballast hostage
for a while, jailed in the pages of your magazine.

In a nutshell, dear poetry editor,
I submit my anxiety to your forthcoming issue.
Yet, for now, I refuse to submit to my anxiety issues.

＊

The Grim Reaper and the Empress

The morning crow rattles me again, I'm plucked
from the branch of the cherry tree I used to climb,
lanky-boned and wild, under the heron-eye
of gnarled grandpapa. It was felled long after you left.
Blue ivy wound its mist around the barks, bending
the stubborn crown, the flowerbeds fouling
in November rain. Inside your fear I heard
at the brain-basement note of that shivering howl
a harmonica, yellowed by wiser lips, and the count
of foreign numbers: one, two, tree. Ghosts from a wasted
sharpness of mind, reaping seeds from the soil.
Yesterday, in the cinnamon-scent of your kitchen,
Kafka echoed in our mugs: *On the moonlight square a man
walks still ahead in the snow.* We lit the boding candle,
it rounded his moon-face in the grayscale photograph
your daughter framed in gold.
Dust kept falling on the scrubbed pane
like a thin fog on mountain range. I couldn't
see him. There was no life, just light, thrown on the still
bridging our world and the old. He only visits me,
I told you, in my sleep. Until dusk
we sat together, caught in the rising flame,
looks into the evening water, hands on old stones—
a fierce love pinched me in the gut, and secateurs
severing the rotten tendrils. There, under wilted leaves,
a fresh shoot crawling out to spring, and your dewy eyes.

Hay Fever

It came upon me like a thunderstorm, sudden and quick:
I couldn't walk the streets safely, but I was used to it.

This time I was swollen and kept swelling through spring,
my strawberry-eyes mashed and moist, itching with ire.

The nose was the worst: it quickened its sprints
until it lay half-dead, barely able to catch a breath.

From behind my bedroom window I watched the mist
conquer my street: sunflower-yellow, feigning softness,

pollinating cars and bins and toys, settling down
as a rug subtler than light in every slit, corner and crack.

My doctor said this is what happens when male trees
are planted without thirsty females to suck up their pollen.

As these hazardous clouds of yellow swirl by, my boiling
tomato head thumps and pounds, thinks of my mum,

who lowered her hot head in the streets, crossing men
having the craic— she pretended not to see them.

And I remember how her cheeks caught fire in church
when the congregation passed through the aisle,

the priest swinging his censer, menacing the Holy Spirit
to take shape at any moment. My mother's doe eyes fell

to the floor then, pretending that she never saw his shadow-
casting cedar in the back garden, her memories never stained

by the wind-swept pollen on her skin.

Cooking Class

The neurologist on the podcast tells me that women
are three times more likely than men to get multiple
sclerosis. And orgasms, I think and stuff the chicken.
My mother has one but not the other, last summer
she could barely taste our coq au vin.
I chop my veg and oil your sweet potato fries,
watch you tapping your phone, moving stocks
and bonds on the broker app I assume from the coin
shape your lips form in concentration. Seen from a female
gaze, your cock winds itself in your tracksuit pants
like a temptress or the snake of sin.
If you were cooking, I'd go down on you, risk
burning our meal. I wouldn't mind at all
if you came over and fucked me here right now.
The doctor says it's women's high levels
of stress which make them more vulnerable
to developing MS, not so much their DNA.
I wonder if stress is not hereditary, too,
and what we could do about it. With cream
cheesed hands I shove the chicken in the oven.

Composition X: Vasily Kandinsky, 1939

The tsar commands the expansion of space.
        Stretch the darkness across the edges, pull taut
            the skin where the crescent moon is waning. Shoot
    your friend in the eye when it bloodies at the green.

The tsar commands the killing of time.
        Coop up the bibles and bribes in a puddle, rest assured
            in the staccato crotchets of the weeping Domra. Halt
    the blue rider in its straitjacket when it neighs too much noise.

The tsar commands the extinction of light.
        Mute the vibrant colours of every lip and lover, sever
            the tails from float, fish and foe. Square
    all circles and draw lines between dead bodies.

The tsar commands the spreading of seeds.
        You think to plant a hook here, heather over there, dig deep
            into the earth's bunker and pull out roots. You will swallow
    magma and spit it out into the hunting darkness.

Instructions for Matting the Shine of Your Hair

All I can do to hide is braid my hair. Weave in threads of grey with a thin streak of blue, like the Irish sky— forever mercurial. I wear those threads in my braids when I go out. In blossom-bright parks, running tracks flooded by light on wintry nights, and leafy paths snaking alongside rivers. I see the threads in little girls' flying plaits. Mothers' manes curling down their backs. Wise women's silver dappled with the colours that bind us together. A woman warned us in an online forum: *Man jerked off at 7:45 pm on canal between Bridge Street and Wolfe Tone Bridge.* Male commenters take offence to her Canadian English: men in Ireland don't *jerk off,* but the guy is surely a *wanker.* They crack jokes, shoot poisoned arrows at the creator of the post. Women ask what he looked like; after three hours they've identified three different offenders across town. Locations to practise caution in are exchanged. Words of blue and grey: *so sorry this happened to you, I've seen it too.* The Gardaí have been informed. One comment snaps my breath: *Would you guys laugh if your mother, wife, or daughter passed a man jerking himself off in public?* She doesn't get a response. I jump in my running clothes and braid my hair. Blonde, blue, grey — lapping over and stringing into a bouncing rope, thickening with each story I hear. I don't want to be scared. *Rape culture is alive and well,* the woman closes the thread. We, with our blue and grey streaks, continue our rounds outside, looking for each other. Weaving, braiding, and no hair tie to fasten the end.

The dream in which I cut my comfort blanket into leaves

The monkey cage stinks against the wind. Its back
door falls open   towards the planetarium. What
would I do if they came for me?   The legs only
sprint   as far as fear   treetops look like crowns
when sun plays   with their leaves   monkeys pee
from heights   screech at us   perhaps laughing.

I sit at a table and order a latte; an ape
slaps his hand on my thigh and grins.
You should write a pamphlet about crap,
and name it "Education". Thank me later.

The summer when I put my hand through the fence
and nearly lost it to a vulture   flesh in the shape
of a shattered star   pink   like a steak; the winter
I confused   the swing   with a slide   falling
in mud   the pigs' eyes on my shame   frostbitten
nose   and no one to get me   to my purpling feet.

For years I marched against zoos   almost
I would've become a keeper. But for whom.

I am your ache, the ape says, *thank me later.*

Someday I will run 26 miles in a circle
not bigger   than the rim   of his eye.

A beetle lands on the biscuit wrapping. I tell the ape
the dream of my triumph: I no longer   need sweets
unwrap my nipples   give milk   no poem in me —
the ape sits in the chair across from me   and waits.

The Bathtub

To say that you do wonders
is a bit of an understatement.

I found you in the shop on the corner—
Furey's little hardware store.

You were getting LED lightbulbs while
I was lugging a bag of Polish coal.

You like to get your hands dirty? you smiled,
and I didn't know what you meant exactly,

so I nodded. *I know, but it keeps the house warm,*
my lips apologised, wanting to lock onto yours.

You've since installed some electric heaters,
and when you climbed into the bathtub with me

the other day, I knew that you loved me.
I apologise for telling you often that

I don't really matter, that the world won't end
with me rushing about, blowing poison into the trees,

because you've shown me that I do
actually matter, and the distance

between us at the kitchen table
is far too wide.

Apus

β

δ

γ

α

ε

η

———————————

β The woods run me more than I run in them. I circle trees, slip on mud; after a breeze I can barely feel my feet. I'm panting, soaring as if puppeteered from above

γ but not flying. The branches beneath me crack and crunch under this force my body will not incorporate. Lavatic lungs catapult me into an opening—

δ pause for a minute, gather my breaths, expand the belly. A dark shape shoots past and shadows a trembling fawn, reproachful clacking of the hooves. Fort of twigs and stems. Her golden eyes on me

α and day after day strung together as pearls on a choker necklace. Red mushrooms pierce through moss as my knees bend, sink fingers into dewy cushions. My eyes tending towards the earthy ε   and navel gazing. I'm dragged on to cross the clearing, back under the chilly crown of leaves. Pounding wings that never spread, feet cut off to trap something free and beautiful. My legs still carry me

η   through this skinniness, back into the palm of your hand at nights by the lake. Campfire bread on a stick, you and I naked under a sparkling sky. Stargazing, you say, is wishing yourself small and magical.

Rupture, Patch

The sheep couldn't glean much
from the footprints cast in mud.
It's not the fox or the tame wolf,
king Billy calms his flock,
probably the two-legged gobshite.
Eyes roll around the slope,
choir of resigned bleating.
Benbulben's recent splitting
sent thunder across the rocks,
mothers reported lambs missing,
and some big-footed erosions.
We never fall from the steep tip,
but following strangers' breadcrumbs
lands us in deadly trouble, Billy warns.
Fairy tales are only plates, holding
those who crave meat and cheese,
but the mountain is a green
table, laid for a feast of grass.
Let us stay here, the king commands,
this shall be our holy ruminating place.

Tomatoes

I've always wanted someone who grows tomatoes
like earlobes. You braid the vines together, a plait
of spikes and tentacles. Reaching for plump
fruit, juicing and slushing; each summer my lust
and your green fingers find each other
even on the coarsest soils, on graves of cracking
earth. There are nights when my tongue curls
around the snail of your ear, and then some days
you plough my fields with rigour and stern.
By the end of summer, there would always be
tomato, ripe and fleshy and dripping.
My teeth sink into the peel and tear it like
wrapping paper, whereas your lips close
around the puckering shape. I would then sigh
and call you *garden witch,* and gift you
the soft gum and warm of a kiss for growing.

Observations from a Restaurant

I sit and inspect the cutlery placed before me. The engraving on the knife says *utopia*. That strikes me as odd. I consult the dictionary:

Utopia: noun
- often capitalized: a place of ideal perfection especially in laws, government, and social conditions
- an impractical scheme for social improvement
- an imaginary and indefinitely remote place

Etymology
Utopia, imaginary and ideal country in *Utopia* (1516) by Sir Thomas More, from Greek *ou* not, no + *topos* place

———————

The main course interrupts my research. Utopia strips chunks of meat from chicken wings, baring bone by bone. Have you ever seen a skeleton fly?

The animal's flesh goes no place, or a remote place.

Utopia sleeps on my serviette, greasy with greed, but of course it's not really there, it must all be a figment of my imagination.

No, this is a knife. What *is* a knife?

———————

Knife: noun
1. a) a cutting instrument consisting of a sharp blade fastened to a handle
    b) a weapon or tool resembling a knife

2. a sharp cutting blade or tool in a machine

verb
- to use a knife on, *specifically*: to stab, slash, or wound with a knife
- to cut, mark, or spread with a knife
- to try to defeat by underhanded means
- to move like a knife in, *example*: birds knifing the autumn sky

_____

If birds knife the sky, and utopia knifes the bird, then I guess it all makes perfect sense, don't you think?

The waiter takes the knife, *Utopia*, away.

My tummy rumbles and mumbles on.

Outside, a swarm of starlings race towards a fireball— together, they sink into the sea.

Pink Tram Line to Margaretenstraße

after Rosamund Taylor

Night's sour spitting: empty tram waiting
to leave Spandau— littered seats, pissing
rain. I press my back against the window and hold
my breath. Until Bellevue, floodlights chasing

my shadow and you. No one home but an unloving
God, forging walls of air: crisp here, outskirts reeking. Berlin
Mitte: concrete bricks tower into clouds, mouthless
screams, in tongues from wet soil. And you, cold

nose buried in my neck, whisper the names of girls:
Anne, Zeynep, Saoirse. We board the S1 to Lichterfelde
West, where streetlamps like torches light the path
to your home, and the tunnel gushes

past, unbending as our pink line of sight, your lips
the colour of it: this sunrise is holy and ours.

Scrabbling

Like John Dee spoke to the angels
        I ask you what keeps me
orbiting. Perhaps it's the Espresso

Martini you're sipping, you say.
You're not talking to a jester,
I'm a serious poet, no degree

in writing but my Mercury snuggles
        up to my sun, on the cusp
of melancholic Pisces. I have a word

with you, and pick on the angel wings
gracing my cocktail. It wasn't a model
who first had this drink, who believes

such tails. I sulk over the dry sand-
        wiches on my plate.
A good sandwich needs more greens,

you say, and thick glazed ham. A girl
        should be aloud
to sink her teeth in, but I'm a grown

womban, so I stick my lips to the rim
of my glass, glossed in nude. Our scrying
board is the cocktail menu. You throw

a coin: it whirls and lands on hex
        on the beach— dee angels
have answered. I shake their words

into a poem and pour it in your mouth,
        you sun of a pitch-
black universe, letting me spin.

Dublin Elegy

Well, that's Dublin, my sister says,
her sandpaper-voice scratching

through the phone. I lullaby
myself more than her, scanning the blood-starred

road ahead of me for brake lights, but the car trail
speeds into night. I arrive and she shows me her room: first

floor, overlooking the back garden
and bins. The guy next door sucks

phlegm up from his lungs like a buck's
breeding call, once, twice, thrice. The kitchen floor

speckled with cornflakes, the roofer housemate's
boot profile cast in mud in the hall. *I'll live*

like this forever, she says, *I'll never earn
enough for my own place.* My tongue runs

over teeth, looking for word crumbs, and find
the fact that my partner owns a house

as a raspberry seed stuck in my molar. Without
him I'd be renting a shoebox. *But the sea*

isn't far from here, she says, half-looking out the moonlit
window, her gaze catching a leaf tumbling from the crown

of the trembling elm — behind it another house,
all windows shut with blinds.

When he brushed my hair I knew I loved him

for John

If you must
I will   still
letting you brush
warm blow   upon me
made   to be soft
on a body   steeled
but here   with me
I am a girl   again
candle   melting

                      yes,

                              yes

make me   a mother
I sit on the bed
my hair   and the wind's
your fingers and mouth
innocent   blooms
by a man's   voice
you are silk and cloud
but safe   and waxen
flickering

and I wish
braid   this bed
like I weave
around yours   in dreams
but my hair is not
night   I misplace
wade   swollen
and burn   my feet
glow
that I lost   fear
                      the tight
                            plait

I would
into my hair
my legs
of wet   ember
grippy   in this snow-lit
sleep   and sperm
through white
in the cold
knowing
and I don't need it

The Killing Kind

As I'm speeding on the N4 to Sligo, heading to my sunset
       yoga at the beach, the trees bent
under fiery clouds, I see a Badger spreading over the asphalt,

       on the edge of the white
line severing grey and green.

A neutral voice on the radio tells me that women's
       wombs are being combed now in the States,
seeking for living crumbs in every egg,

       while Wolves and Orangutans crumple
their stomachs into little balls of cosmic dust, sinking stars,

but the voice doesn't tell me that, it's just in my head,
       like a hammer on the pit of a cherry. They quickly move on
to the war that's raging in Europe: at home, my people

       are scared again, *What if the bullets patter upon us next?*
Berlin isn't so far from Kyiv, hushed screams or roaring whispers.

Berlin is *schön schrecklich*, but I love my Münster; the first settlers
       called it Monstre, an honest name at least
for something built by humankind, its pretty bourgeoisie a shroud

       for the unseeable, the stiff collars a pillar
of consensual myopia.

I pass a cemetery and think of all the Badgers, Foxes, Martens,
       Deer that should be mourned
right here, or someplace,

       and that my car should be boasting
a black cross, this coffin.

Violence in Gaza, rising oil prices, inflation,
I'm going to freeze in the winter, they say, yet here I am,
spilling into the sunset, with wind-wet eyes, blood-firing heart,

and I'm still not on the pill.

On Enniscrone Beach with my Mother

Fishhook and crunching shells. Salt
etched in foam by winter sun; your hand
ploughing the beach for stones that fit
in your palm and skip on sea. I don't know
how the ocean washed at our feet a string
of green to sew our rags into a warming
quilt. We use your new sewing machine—
you put your foot down and guide the thread
with hands like rails. If we met in my dream
you'd wear your old brown leggings that wrapped
around your Rubens thighs. You loved them
despite their heavy pilling, a dirty
stubble, and I laughed at you
for keeping them. You might be
scolding me, your pointer finger
in the air. I didn't like your sandpaper
frown but I loved your strength. Now, on this mild
December day, your dopamine pills rush ashore
an untamed girl with pearly eyes. Somehow
your skin won't wrinkle, although your twiggy
legs shuffle and stall by night. You're not
trembling much, just soft and fine feather
clouds at the horizon. *Look around,* you say
at the height of your high, *how beautiful this is.*

Acknowledgements

Thank you to the editors of the following journals and presses that published poems from this book, sometimes in earlier versions:

Anthropocene Poetry, époque press, fifth wheel, Full House Lit, Ink Sweat & Tears, Gone Lawn, Kelp Journal, lean and loafe, Luain Press, MAYDAY, MORIA, Needle Poetry, New Isles Press, Poetry Ireland Review, Poetry Salzburg Review, Poetry Wales, Skylight 47, The Moth, Southword, The Selkie, The Stony Thursday Book, Tír na nÓg, untethered, York Literary Review.

'Party Politics' won the Luain Press Poetry Competition (2022).

'Solitary/Riverbed' was highly commended in The Black Cat Press's Nature Poetry Competition 2024.

'The Killing Kind' was longlisted in The National Poetry Competition (2022).

Some poems appeared in my chapbook *Leafing* (2024), which won the Cerasus Poetry Chapbook Competition.

Many thanks to Grace Wilentz & Gallery Press and Patrick Cotter & Munster Literature Centre for giving me the opportunity to hone my craft in their workshops, in which I first drafted some of the poems in this book.

Much gratitude to Arts Council Ireland for funding my work with an Agility Award, and to my mentor Rebecca Goss, who helped me shape some of these poems and gave me a fresh perspective on this collection.

The Author

Christina Hennemann (www.christinahennemann.com) is a poet and writer. Her work has been supported by Arts Council Ireland and Mayo County Council. She received the Luain Press Poetry Prize and the Diana Woods Memorial Award in Creative Nonfiction. She was selected for the National Mentoring Programme and the Freedom to Write Award. Her poems appear in *Poetry Ireland, Poetry Wales, Southword, Poetry Salzburg Review*, and elsewhere.

www.ingramcontent.com/pod-product-compliance
Lightning Source LLC
Chambersburg PA
CBHW050015090426
42734CB00020B/3274